Around the Lake

poems by

Mo Corleone

Finishing Line Press
Georgetown, Kentucky

Around the Lake

Copyright © 2021 by Mo Corleone
ISBN 978-1-64662-511-6 First Edition
All rights reserved under International and Pan-American Copyright Conventions. No part of this book may be reproduced in any manner whatsoever without written permission from the publisher, except in the case of brief quotations embodied in critical articles and reviews.

Publisher: Leah Huete de Maines

Editor: Christen Kincaid

Cover Art: Mo Corleone

Author Photo: Mo Corleone

Cover Design: Elizabeth Maines McCleavy

Order online: www.finishinglinepress.com
        also available on amazon.com

Author inquiries and mail orders:
Finishing Line Press
PO Box 1626
Georgetown, Kentucky 40324
USA

Table of Contents

Three Blocks 1

No Peace 2

Take Care 4

The Drummers 5

36 Stolen 6

Coronatrends 2020 7

Rugged Individual 8

Bold 9

Door No. 2 10

The Sun Did Not Rest 11

Law and Order 12

Burn It Down 13

Stay Underground 14

Colonial Legacy 16

June Third 17

Revolutions 18

Message Scent 19

What I Can and Cannot Say To Héctor 20

Flash Bang 22

Salvation 23

Notes 24

*To the citizens of Oakland
and those who stand in solidarity
All power to the people*

Three Blocks

in the 5:00 hour
on a weekday
around the lake
three blocks makes all the difference

near grand and macarthur
beside the freeway
against the melee
say a prayer at the white light crossing

before thinking
without a care for a future
beyond that onramp
they <u>will</u> hit and run you

up the short hill
despite only three blocks distance
at a stop sign in adams point
you go. no, please—you go.

No Peace

the noise is impossible to tune out
chugging churning thunder rumbling freeway
a chemical reaction is instant, constant
i may never find a moment's peace in this place

chugging churning thunder rumbling freeway
roiling, ripping into my awareness
i may never find a moment's peace in this place
now that i detect this provocation

roiling, ripping into my awareness
are mirrors these insulting sounds reflect
now that i detect this provocation
absurd to turn the ugliness down and pretend

are mirrors these insulting sounds reflect
reminders of my own internal din?
absurd to turn the ugliness down and pretend
face it to change it, face it to change it

reminders of my own internal din
wishes resisted to drown out the soundtrack
face it to change it, face it to change it
can't just take a longer lake walk, make the tape pop

wishes resisted to drown out the soundtrack
the humbling, heavy truth of right response
can't just take a longer lake walk, make the tape pop
no lessons learned in trying to deny it

the humbling, heavy truth of right response
admit the program playing now is racist
no lessons learned in trying to deny it
i hear it running scripts inside my head unchecked

admit the program playing now is racist
the noise is impossible to tune out
i hear it running scripts inside my head unchecked
a chemical reaction is instant, constant

Take Care

the intermittent tents loosely holding the unhoused
remind me there is nothing guaranteed, forge ahead carefully

sat close enough to hear a high-speed blowout on 580
and terror from the tearing of the tires not sped carefully

a helicopter roar irritating to my core
i'm fortified for fights from adrenaline, undead carefully

some motorcycles feature the exhaust of antisocials
no helmet since the rider chose to flash and then bled carefully

my music practice answers with the impulse to be loudest
adjust the volume down and be respectful instead carefully

each blossom on the sidewalk joyful teardrops from a tree
i softly walk around—nature prevails if i tread carefully

The Drummers

some remind me of cormorants
holding court near the columns
an air of dignity blessing their proceedings
rhythm in council and community

one is like the canada geese
sprawling as if calling the space, ever greedy
a curse of inescapable fragrant flagrance
assaulting senses with impunity

i long to laud the lot of them
knowing all wildlife needs refuge, safe habitat
(all of us) we make room at this tidal lagoon
but fuck you, geese. lost opportunity.

36 Stolen

one friend safely outside
rushing back indoors to warn
to save, to fail,
to bury the treasure of a thousand half-formed masterpieces.

one bold and sweet creator
held in my heart, the soft revolutionary
clinging to his love
in a pompeii embrace.

and the lover, ever sparkling
scintillant in possibility
talent bubbling over, joyous
a choking caress is no consolation.

one desk in the office
the effusive new engineer used to sit here
flowers and heartbreak instead
shadowed beneath a cloud of disbelief.

red tape for solutions
red carpet for the monster among us
red alert for atrocity at his doorstep
ready or not, it's done.

you who adds gall upon appalling
with your hollow offer to tattoo the 36 stolen:
accept in lieu 36 candles to illuminate your betrayal,
and 36 sentences with missing periods

Coronatrends 2020

sparse are the models on the runway
six feet measures distance, not height

the loneliest flaunting of this season's looks
heretofore unseen

solos and pairs only
locking eyes with those who dare this same minute

masks care a lot less than
mascara, hot from this collection:

the lost monopoly of the rich
on taking more than what is needed

calling your mom
per the schedule of her secret dreams

washing your hands
the way that makes her and the scientists proud

shouting encouragement at familiar features
a friend's shape running around the lake

Rugged Individual

you emerged from subdivision monoculture
having scored no songs, painted no canvas,
penned zero works either great or average

issued a single holy book of moral codes
with a box of kindergarten zombie crayons
pretending you could color outside the lines

a flannel-lined designer suburban cage
reckless echoes of replicated news programs
manipulated algorithm lullaby lambs

seatbelt fastened in predictable pickup
satisfactorily masculine by classic standards
acceptable regard for speed limits in traffic

blind to scripted wages of war and labor
sleepwalk, racing the clock, chasing a dollar
the threat of a jail cell a covert shock collar

yet we find you loud in the crowded store
retailing, assailing shoppers, wailing
railing against masks as an instrument of control

Bold

by quarantine standards
a trio of men outdoors is bold
from the back, surely spurning guidance
from the front, obvious blood family

even more audacious
one man alone
ostensibly following rules
steers a dented car into a median tree

turns on hazard lights
people should watch out here
watch the driver open the door
wide and wander away

pants have long fled the waist
indeed everything is escaping
remnants of life spilling from his wallet
fluttering in the wind

Door No. 2

surely we understand in the end
the earth will prevail, but in what form?
nature will force its abusers through
one of three doors
today: door number 2—*disease*

on shores of lakes, from merritt to biwa
will a beacon of soft flute melody
guide those of us remaining
to take our seats in the cradle
of tree branches and form a new council?

today: mask on, six feet distant
i am not afraid.
only grateful to sit quietly on the grass
contemplating the alternatives of hard reset
    war   famine

thank you, nature
behind this door, we can manage
adjust and appreciate
even the geese have thinned to just two
pleasant, pecking, plucking.

The Sun Did Not Rest

called this the day the sun didn't rise
another way that tales are lies
star regardless rules our skies
even when smoke is dense
face our consequence
stinging, immense
tangerine
citrine
scene

Law and Order

Acting as if every person incarcerated
belongs behind bars because
criminals scare you senseless
doesn't void reality, doesn't grant humanity
Everybody knows a bad guy
Fear and finance, fat and feeding
gorged on just desserts and pious pie
Hardcoded holes in the Constitution
Injustice served with precise intention
Jury jettisoned, took the plea for a chance
killed the soul but kept the back strong
Labor cheap lines pockets, keeps shelves stocked
My daddy once told me there was
no such thing as rehabilitation for the hardened;
only suicide proves true remorse.
Peonage will do in a pinch, presumably—don't
question the motives, eyes on the prizes:
Removal from society, illusion of safety
Servitude, subjugation, slavery substitute
Treat mere existence as reason to seize
Ugly side brandished and clutching the keys
Votes don't count, voice choked out
We all remember a bad guy, right?
X-cons for life
Youth and adult—felons as predicted
Zero tolerance for pretend offenders

Burn It Down

"nothing would fundamentally change"
unless, of course,
the rippling aqua dragon skin
of this breezy lake surface
rises from intolerable agony
boiling in the beast beneath
forces upward ancient wings
mountain scabs cracking open
heaving out of hibernation
twin sky lungs
one deep and dutiful breath
delivering the hero we need
fire
scorching, final
fire.

Stay Underground

Dear Libby, hope you're well
and by that I mean
rot in hell
Can't believe I fell for your
cheerleader hills spell

Don't talk to me at work
how you love Oakland
You and Aaron both can drum up
dicks on choke

I forgive zero
of your endless pretending
pretentious ilk, how'd you figure I'd be
defending your brand
which is woke white fakers
using optics as the upper hand

Fooled me twice
with your permit fees like a mark
Now I break my own heart
voting no against the Parks
and Youth Development
we all know what you meant
when you said "development"—
Corporate.
Crazy rent.

But I'm the master of the last laugh
Don't need permission
I'll be pissing on your epitaph

One lake vigil (crock)
does not check the box
Our pain is still alive
Our artwork's the mock up and talks

You can't destroy our dreams
with deployment of teams
erasing all the paintings
candles flowers screams

Keep the columns squeaky clean
Say debris to demean
Grief is banished, homeless stay
I don't care what you say
It's not your land anyway

Colonial Legacy

a miracle the indigenous
will entertain our thousandth chance
abandoned treaties, stolen
land mere product for johns
adams, sutter, muir...
kill, degrade, chain
still the same
i feel
shame

June Third

your calendar is wrong
today isn't about me and i see
your wishes but i won't hear them over
the helicopters and the defiance

your spotlight is misdirected
my ire is outward-focused and i see
you mean well choosing side issues over
tyrant demise—all eyes on the uprising!

your priorities are scrambled
i know this judgment hurts you, i see.
you're still my friend and love, it's not over
let's heal later—deeper wounds are calling

my soul is rattled from battle
true justice may not be something i see
in this life. breeze in trees, blow me over
i'm trapped in attacks while praying for peace

Revolutions

i am so sorry baby to wreck
your birthday but there will be more
revolutions around the
sun and just one blazing
revolution, here,
now, to demand
justice in
this crazed
world

Message Scent

smell my resistance t-shirt
faint trace of tear gas
and wild armpit
just how you like it

time to stand up
wave cresting, one voice rising
fists in electric air
even our hair stands up

What I Can and Cannot Say to Héctor

A friendly *hola* tumbles out
a casual assumption on my part
welcomed, returned so genuinely
I gamble on a stranger exchange

Likely unwise, a sidewalk stowaway
but his smiling eyes are true and kind
I answer with truth instinctively
Voy a caminar a Lake Merritt

When he asks permission to join
I oblige, try atrophied Spanish
¿De donde eres? (México)
¿Y donde vives? (pointing: *allí, allí, allí...*)

His meaning makes it through
alrededor del lago
The stories stay buried in thousands
of wrinkles sculpted by sunblast

Linguistic limits laughable
we hobble with contrasting handicaps
still, certain subjects are universal
violencia de la policía

Makeshift queer ballroom event
our lakeside amphitheater greeting
No school, no restaurant had prepared me
My best: "gay dance with judges"

The depth of understanding of consent
in his response, the opposite of macho
vastly more beautiful than my takeaway
me gusta, te gusta, no problema

Neither can I translate the pride prize—too real
a taser in a purse for self-defense
Creo que el mundo sería mejor sin violencia
I wish I could tell him we all agree

Flash Bang

to a DJ
flash bang
is a sound and lights production

to the media
flash bang
is a whimsical woo-hoo, a lollipop

from the police line
flash bang
is a grenade and nothing else

from the party line
the flippant term "less-lethal"
you'll live

Salvation

open arms of the mountain panorama
radiate love that laps in waves, audible
breathe in the presence of spirit here
ancestors rebirthed as cloud and clover

urban harms of a people drowned in progress
severed from truth—ensnared, enslaved, gullible
leave it behind when its grip slips here
melodies reclaimed by hum and strumming

mental strands tie these moments softly dreaming
validate flesh, discerning mind, provable
oh where we go when aloft of here
memories remade abstracted over

gentle hands understanding felt like fiction
liquid reprieve transforms the wall, movable
merge with the water for healing here
blessed rescue at long last is coming

Notes

No Peace
"It is difficult to dispute the conclusion that the victims of highway construction and routing were predominantly poor, minority urban residents. Many also argue that highways were routed through black neighborhoods in a routine and purposeful manner, claims that are supported in part by planning documents and revisions in many American cities. Many have alleged that such decisions connect to organized efforts among public officials to maintain lines of residential segregation and discrimination, and to support efforts to rid central city neighborhoods of minority communities. While this is perhaps more pronounced in some cities than others, scholars have concluded that it was the explicit attempt of highway planners to achieve discriminatory results" (Rose & Mohl, 2012).
> -New Visions for Public Affairs, *Highway to Inequity: The Disparate Impact of the Interstate Highway System on Poor and Minority Communities in American Cities*

Public health experts agree that environmental risks constitute 25% of the burden of disease. Widespread exposure to environmental noise from road, rail, airports and industrial sites contributes to this burden. [...] Noise pollution is considered not only an environmental nuisance but also a threat to public health.
> -World Health Organization, *Burden of disease from environmental noise*

36 Stolen
On December 2, 2016, the Ghost Ship warehouse fire claimed 36 lives. A tragedy by any measurement, the loss was felt deeply in Oakland's underground dance music scene.

"...for many of us, these spaces are what have kept us alive. In a world that demands its inhabitants to be a certain way, think a certain way, or live a certain way, we gravitate to the spaces that say: Welcome. Be yourself. For the tormented queer, the bullied punk, the beaten trans, the spat-upon white trash, the disenfranchised immigrants and young people of color, these spaces are a haven of understanding in a world that doesn't understand—or can't, or doesn't seem to want to try.

    -Gabe Meline, *It Could Have Been Any One Of Us*,
    kqed.org

The Sun Did Not Rest
On September 9, 2020, the Bay Area skies were so choked by wildfire smoke and ash that the sky stayed dark all day. The Air Quality Index (AQI) ratings in multiple West Coast locations in September were so high they no longer registered on the charts.

Stay Underground
Libby Schaaf is the current Mayor of Oakland, California.

Mo Corleone was born and raised in Sacramento but truly brought to life as an adult in the major cities of California's bustling Bay Area. Performing and signing autographs since the age of 7, Mo enjoyed an early introduction to theatre, Shakespeare festivals, poetry readings, and music through an exceptional program in a public school. Her creative engine has continued to fire on multiple cylinders, fueled by the constant inspiration of her surroundings and a runaway imagination.

In the decades that followed, Mo developed (and soothed) herself through artistic pursuits like singing songs, acting in plays, painting watercolors, drawing birds, practicing instruments, rocking dance floors as a DJ, composing electronic music, and of course writing poems. Without such balms, she may not have survived some of the more violent and difficult years.

Around the Lake reflects one active citizen's perspective on people, pandemic, and protests. It earned an honorable mention in the LGBTQ Chapbook Contest sponsored by The Southern Collective Experience, but readers may notice matters of sexuality, gender, and race are largely absent from the work. Mo's ambiguous place on those spectra has led to deep experience in a gray area, deftly passing for whatever the situation deemed necessary (white, straight, stable, etc.) and she is still learning to embrace her true identity as 'Other'. Consequently, the critically important storytelling by marginalized communities is deferred with respect to those expert voices. Mo remains committed to speaking up and speaking out but draws a boundary at speaking *for* anyone but herself.

www.ingramcontent.com/pod-product-compliance
Lightning Source LLC
LaVergne TN
LVHW041515070426
835507LV00012B/1582